THE ANCIENT
Near East

THE ANCIENT Near East

REBECCA STEFOFF

BENCHMARK BOOKS

MARSHALL CAVENDISH
NEW YORK

AUTHOR'S NOTE ON DATES

This book covers thousands of years, starting in prehistory, before the people of the ancient Near East had invented written languages. Even after they started writing down their history, however, they did not record everything, and many of the records they *did* make have not survived to modern times. We do not always know exactly when an ancient event occurred. Some dates are simply the best guesses that historians can make, using the most accurate information available.

All of the dates in this book fall within the time period now called B.C.E. (for Before the Common Era). B.C.E. dates are numbered backward from the year 1, which marks the beginning of the Common Era (or C.E.) a little more than two thousand years ago. When you are dealing with B.C.E. dates, remember that higher numbers are longer ago than lower numbers. To find out how long ago an ancient event occurred, add today's year to the B.C.E. date of that event. For example, if you are reading this book in the year 2007, and you learn that a people called the Hyksos invaded Egypt around 1630 B.C.E., add 2007 to 1630. You'll find that the invasion took place roughly 3,637 years before 2007.

Benchmark Books · Marshall Cavendish Corporation · 99 White Plains Road · Tarrytown, New York 10591-9001
www.marshallcavendish.com · Copyright © 2005 Rebecca Stefoff · All rights reserved. No part of this book may be reproduced or utilized in any form or by any means electronic or mechanical including photocopying, recording, or by any information storage and retrieval system, without permission from the copyright holders. · All Internet sites were available and accurate when sent to press.
· Library of Congress Cataloging-in-Publication Data · Stefoff, Rebecca, 1951– · The ancient Near East / Rebecca Stefoff.
p. cm. — (World historical atlases) • Summary: Text plus historical and contemporary maps provide a look at the history of the Ancient Near East. · Includes bibliographical references and index. · ISBN 0-7614-1639-0
1. Middle East—History—To 622—Juvenile literature. [1. Middle East—History—To 622.] I. Title II. Series:
Stefoff, Rebecca, 1951– · World historical atlases. · DS62.23.S84 2004 · 939′.4—dc22 · 2003012030
Printed in China · 1 3 5 6 4 2 · Book design by: Sonia Chaghatzbanian

Art and photo research by: Linda Sykes Picture Research, Inc., Hilton Head, SC

The photographs in this book are used by permission and through the courtesy of: Bibliotheque Nationale, Paris: front cover; Private Collection/Bridgeman Art Library: ii, 35, 39; Bettmann/Corbis: 6; Dagon Agricultural Collection, Haifa, Israel/Erich Lessing/Art Resource, NY: 8; AKG, London: 11; Louvre, Paris, France/Erich Lessing/Art Resource, NY: 15, 27; British Museum, London/ Bridgeman Art Library, London/NY/Paris: 17; The Art Archive/Archaeological Museum Baghdad/Dagli Orti: 18, back cover; Detroit Institute of Arts: 19; Charles and Josette Lenars/Corbis: 20; Gian Berto Vanni/Corbis: 22; Gianni Dagli Ortii/Corbis: 23, 30; The Granger Collection: 25; The British Museum: 28; Yann Arhus-Bertrand/Corbis: 32; Sandro Vannini/Corbis: 34; Bridgeman Art Library, London/NY/Paris: 37; Museo Egizio, Turin, Italy/Erich Lessing/Art Resource, NY: 38; Egyptian Museum, Cairo/Erich Lessing/Art Resource, NY: 40; Francois Guenet/AKG, London: 41; Rijksmuseum, Leiden, The Netherlands/Erich Lessing/Art Resource, NY: 42

Contents

CHAPTER ONE

Mesopotamia:
Empires and Invasions

Many of the oldest-known writings are records of business and taxation. This ancient clay tablet dates from the third dynasty of the Sumerian city of Ur, between 2113 and 2006 B.C.E. It lists the amounts of grain given to seventeen gardeners in one month. A **scribe** recorded the information by using a stick to press wedge-shaped symbols called cuneiform into the damp clay, which was then allowed to dry.

Civilizations are like towers—they cannot rise until their foundations are in place. Two essential building blocks for any civilization are organized governments and systems of writing. Governments develop when people organize themselves into societies larger and more complex than tribes or villages. Most such societies develop some kind of writing. Government officials use written communication for many things, including tax records and messages to military commanders. But writing also helps societies preserve their histories and cultures. Organized governments and writing seem to have appeared first in the Near Eastern region once known as Mesopotamia, sometimes called a birthplace of civilization.

BEGINNINGS

The name *Mesopotamia* comes from a Greek phrase meaning "between the rivers." Mesopotamia lay between the Tigris and Euphrates rivers in what is now Iraq. It was one of several areas in the Near East where, more than ten thousand years ago, human beings started to give up an age-old way of life for something new.

For many centuries, all people were **nomads** and hunter-gatherers. They moved from place to place in small bands, living on seeds, nuts, honey, wild plants, and wild animals. Then sometime after about 10,000 B.C.E., one group of people started settling down in villages of wood-and-grass huts. Modern **archaeologists** call these people the Natufians. They lived in the Levant, the area at the eastern end of the Mediterranean Sea that now forms the nations Syria, Lebanon, Israel, and Jordan.

Archaeologists once thought that people had not formed permanent settlements until after they had developed agriculture. Discoveries since the 1960s, though, show that the Natufians lived by hunting and gathering. They were not farmers or livestock herders, although they did have one domestic animal, the dog. They also had commerce—their communities traded seashells and carved tools made of bone. The Natufian culture died out around 8000 B.C.E., but by that time two important changes had taken place. First, people in the Levant had begun planting and harvesting grain. Agriculture soon spread throughout the Near East and completely changed

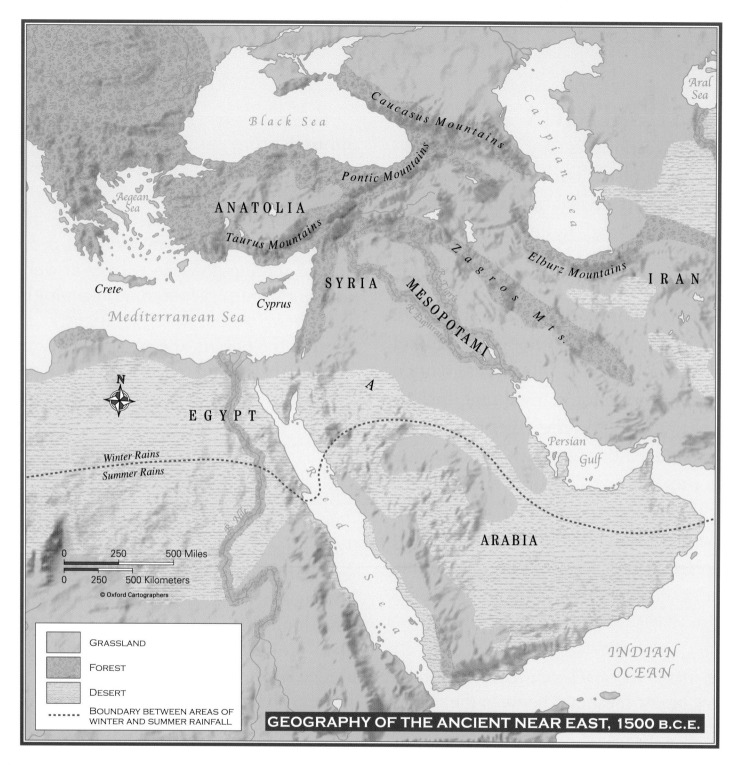

GEOGRAPHY OF THE ANCIENT NEAR EAST, 1500 B.C.E.

Black Sea

Caucasus Mountains

Caspian Sea

Aral Sea

Aegean Sea

Pontic Mountains

ANATOLIA

Taurus Mountains

Zagros Mts.

Elburz Mountains

IRAN

Crete

SYRIA

MESOPOTAMI

Tigris

Cyprus

Mediterranean Sea

R. Euphrates

N

A

EGYPT

Persian Gulf

Winter Rains

Summer Rains

R. Nile

Red Sea

ARABIA

0   250   500 Miles

0   250   500 Kilometers

© Oxford Cartographers

INDIAN OCEAN

GRASSLAND

FOREST

DESERT

BOUNDARY BETWEEN AREAS OF WINTER AND SUMMER RAINFALL

Civilizations took root along the rivers of the ancient Near East, which provided reliable sources of water. People in Mesopotamia and Egypt learned to channel water from their rivers into large canal systems, which irrigated farmland far from the riverbanks. Forests along the region's river valleys provided wood for fuel and building. As towns and cities grew, however, the forests shrank, and wood became scarce. To save their wood for fuel, people turned to other building materials, including stone and bricks made of sun-dried mud and clay.

Priests, such as the one shown praying in this sculpture from the city of Hafaga, played a very important role in Mesopotamian society. They organized the religious life of the city-states. They also helped gather taxes, settle disputes, and spend the money in the royal treasury.

settlements. Surrounded by farmland, these settlements were only small villages— but they would soon give rise to the world's first cities.

THE RISE OF CITY-STATES

Starting around 6000 B.C.E., a handful of villages in southern Mesopotamia grew into the world's first cities. Like the spread of agriculture, the city changed the nature of human life. The first **urban** centers were not only larger than villages, they were more complex in their organization as well. In villages, everyone lived by farming or herding livestock, and everyone had about the same importance in the community. But the cities had craft workers, priests, laborers, and merchants, and they had people of upper and lower classes as well. Cities also served as centers of religious and political life. In fact historians believe that southern Mesopotamia's first cities grew up around sacred shrines or temples.

By about 3500 B.C.E, cities such as Uruk, Ur, and Nippur had grown large enough to control the territory around them. Each urban center was the capital of a city-state, a political unit with an

human life. It freed people from the burden of having to go out in search of food, but at the same time it demanded long hours of hard work. The second change was that people in various parts of the Near East now lived in permanent

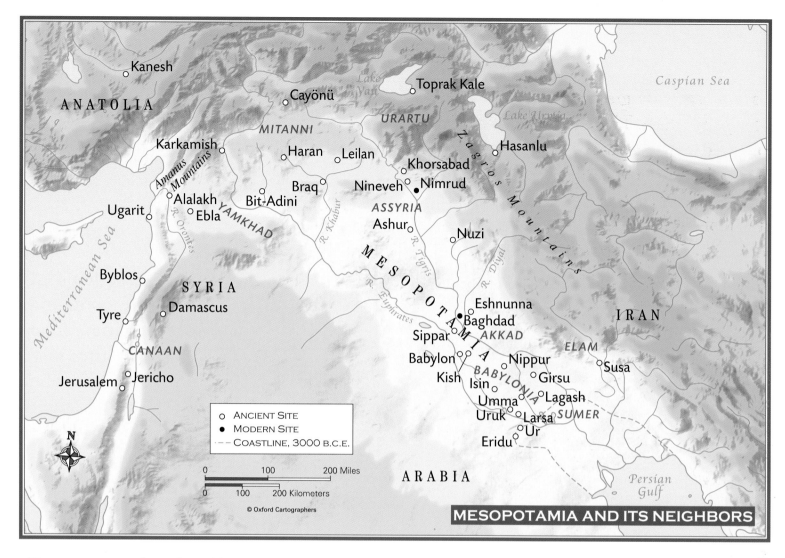

Map labels: Kanesh, Çayönü, Toprak Kale, Caspian Sea, ANATOLIA, Lake Van, URARTU, Lake Urmia, MITANNI, Karkamish, Haran, Leilan, Hasanlu, Zagros Mountains, Khorsabad, Amanus Mountains, Braq, Nineveh, Nimrud, Alalakh, Bit-Adini, ASSYRIA, Ugarit, Ebla, YAMKHAD, R. Khabur, Ashur, Nuzi, R. Orontes, R. Tigris, MESOPOTAMIA, R. Diyala, Mediterranean Sea, Byblos, SYRIA, Eshnunna, IRAN, Tyre, Damascus, R. Euphrates, Baghdad, Sippar, AKKAD, ELAM, CANAAN, Babylon, Nippur, Susa, Jerusalem, Jericho, Kish, BABYLONIA, Girsu, Isin, Lagash, Umma, Uruk, Larsa, SUMER, Eridu, Ur, ARABIA, Persian Gulf

Legend:
○ ANCIENT SITE
● MODERN SITE
--- COASTLINE, 3000 B.C.E.

0   100   200 Miles
0   100   200 Kilometers

© Oxford Cartographers

MESOPOTAMIA AND ITS NEIGHBORS

The great cities of southern Mesopotamia were not the only centers of civilization in the ancient Near East. Jericho, west of Mesopotamia in present-day Jordan, may be the world's oldest town. It dates from the 8000s B.C.E., and although it never became a powerful city-state, people have lived there for about ten thousand years. The largest cities of the time were in Mesopotamia, whose shape has changed since ancient times. The Persian Gulf used to extend much farther inland than it does today (see the dotted line). At their peak, Sumerian cities such as Ur and Lagash were near the seacoast. Over the years, though, the Tigris and Euphrates rivers carried silt down from the highlands, filling in the head of the gulf.

organized government and defined borders. A king ruled each city-state, although priests of the city's special **deity** also held much power. Both the government workers and the priests collected taxes from the people, in the form of food, wool, or other goods, and used them to pay for things such as armies, palaces, and temples. Clerks and priests invented symbols for record keeping, and these eventually grew into the first known form of writing. The oldest surviving traces of writing are clay tablets from about 3300 B.C.E, found in the ruins of Uruk. They are lists of goods, perhaps the contents of a temple's storage rooms. Also from Uruk come the oldest surviving examples of the wheel, which archaeologists think was invented and first used in Mesopotamia.

SUMER AND AKKAD

When the city-states rose to power, southern Mesopotamia was known as Sumer. Although the Sumerian people shared the same language and religion, their various city-states were often at war with each other. In about 2350 B.C.E. the ruler of Umma, one city-state, conquered several other city-states. He was the first to rule over all of Sumer, but his reign did not last. The king of Akkad, a region north of Sumer, invaded Umma and the other Sumerian city-states. He united Sumer and Akkad into a single **empire,** the first to arise in Mesopotamia.

From then on, Mesopotamia's history is marked by the rise and fall of empires. They gained power by conquering their neighbors and lost it when invaded by outsiders. The Akkadian empire, for example,

A New Discovery, An Old Civilization

In 2000 C.E., archaeologists working at Tell Hamoukar in northeastern Syria made a startling announcement: They had uncovered the ruins of a city dating from 3700 to 3500 B.C.E. The discovery is important because scholars have long thought that southern Mesopotamia was the only birthplace of urban civilization. If the scientists working at Tell Hamoukar are right about their find, at least one city already existed in northern Syria when the great ancient cities of southern Mesopotamia were first forming. Located at the northern end of the Tigris and Euphrates River valleys, Tell Hamoukar is part of Mesopotamia, but its urban development was entirely independent of the southern Mesopotamian cities. At Tell Hamoukar a team of archaeologists sponsored by the Syrian government and the University of Chicago has found traces of a large building and a wall that once surrounded the city— evidence that there was a central government that could organize a workforce and oversee a project. Much work is needed before more of the story of Tell Hamoukar is known, but already the find has widened the map of early civilization.

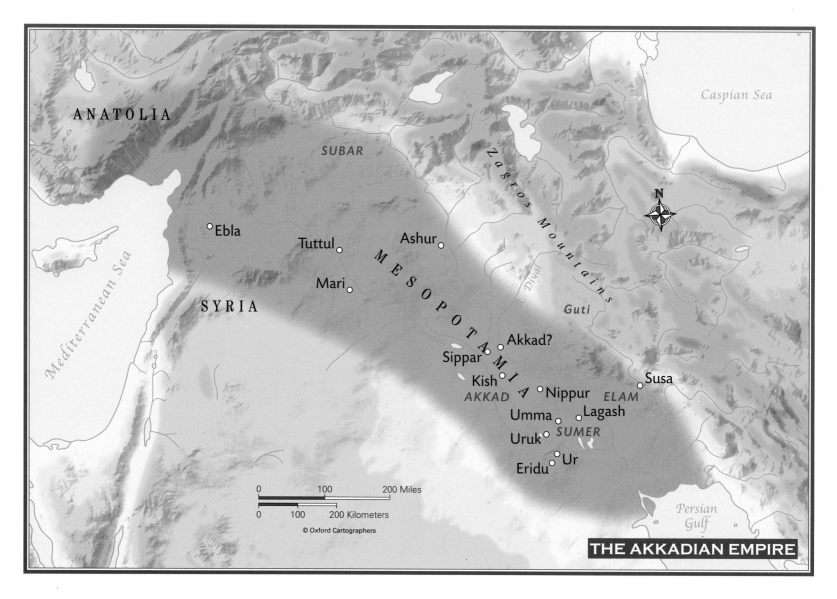

THE AKKADIAN EMPIRE

At its height, the Akkadian empire covered all of Mesopotamia as well as territory to the north. The core of the empire was located in the region called Akkad, home of the rulers. Their capital city, also called Akkad, is one of the great mysteries of Near Eastern archaeology. Its exact location is unknown, and archaeologists have not yet found its ruins.

lasted for two hundred years, only to fall when a nomadic people called the Gutians swarmed over Akkad. Over thousands of years, many hostile armies or roving tribes entered Mesopotamia from beyond its fringes. Flat, fertile, and rich, Mesopotamia had few natural defenses and was a tempting target. Most of the invaders stayed in Mesopotamia and became absorbed into its population and culture.

The First Epic Hero

Some of the world's oldest stories were about a Sumerian hero named Gilgamesh and his remarkable adventures. Around 1700 B.C.E., scribes in Mesopotamia gathered some of these tales into a long poem now known as the *Epic of Gilgamesh*. The most complete surviving version was written on twelve clay tablets around 600 B.C.E. Modern archaeologists found them in the ruins of the Assyrian city of Nineveh. The *Epic of Gilgamesh* tells the story of a warrior king of Uruk who fights a mighty foe named Enkidu. The two admire each other so much that they become friends and set off on adventures that Gilgamesh hopes will bring him everlasting fame. But after Enkidu falls sick and dies, Gilgamesh gives up his quest for fame and searches instead for eternal life. He seeks out a man named Ut-napishtim, who gained eternal life by surviving an ancient flood that drowned the rest of humanity. Ut-napishtim tells Gilgamesh about a plant that gives eternal life. Gilgamesh gets the plant, but a snake steals it from him. The snake eats the plant, sheds its skin, and is reborn into a new and everlasting life. Gilgamesh sadly returns home, having learned that he cannot escape death. At the end of the poem, the ghost of Enkidu visits Gilgamesh to tell him about the world of the dead. The *Epic of Gilgamesh* is one of the oldest known works of literature, but it deals with themes of timeless importance: friendship, death, and the fate of the soul.

The story of the legendary Gilgamesh remained popular in Mesopotamia for several thousand years. This image of the epic hero decorated a palace built in the 700s B.C.E.

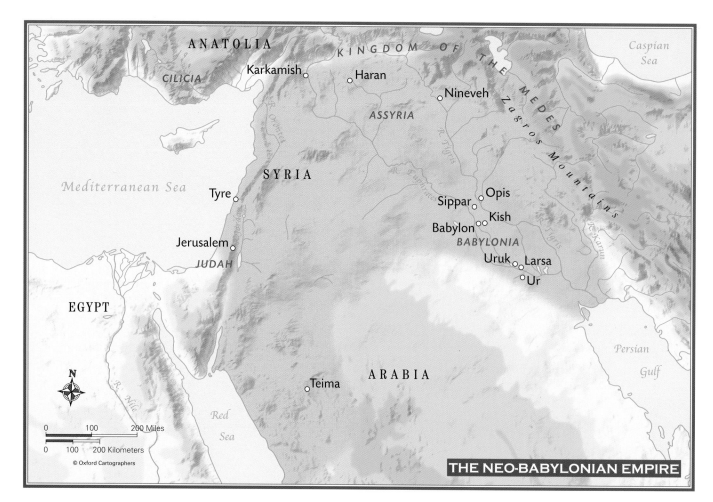

THE NEO-BABYLONIAN EMPIRE

Babylonia rose to power twice in ancient times. The first Babylonian empire thrived between 1900 and 1600 B.C.E. A thousand years later, a new Babylonian power rose in the Near East until the Persians conquered the kingdom in 539 B.C.E. Historians call this second state the Neo-Babylonian empire (*neo* means "new"). It controlled Judah, the ancient kingdom of the Jews, and is the Babylonia mentioned in the Old Testament of the Bible.

BABYLONIA AND ASSYRIA

In time the land of Sumer and Akkad became known as Babylonia. After the fall of Akkad, the region was torn by fighting until a king named Ur-Nammu reunited it under his rule around 2112 B.C.E. A hundred years later, though, Babylonia collapsed after invasions by the Elamites of western Persia (now Iran) and the Amorites, nomads from the Syrian desert. Individual city-states once again became powerful. Then, in the 1760s B.C.E., an Amorite king named Hammurabi forged a new Babylonian empire. Before two centuries had passed, however, Babylonia was overrun by a Persian tribe called the Kassites. The region sank into a dark age of conflict among small, rival kingdoms.

This Babylonian stone map, dating from the period around 700 to 500 B.C.E., was found in the southern part of present-day Iraq. Experts believe it shows parts of both the Babylonian and Assyrian empires as well as the Dead Sea.

Shalmaneser III (left), king of Assyria in the 800s B.C.E., shakes hands with the king of Babylon (right) in a carving from the base of Shalmaneser's throne. Although Shalmaneser III failed to conquer Babylon, later Assyrian kings ruled it for a time.

Meanwhile, north of Babylonia, other Amorite groups had founded a city-state called Ashur. Known as the Assyrians, they grew increasingly powerful, invading and conquering many lands. After 900 B.C.E., under kings such as Sargon II and Ashurbanipal, Assyria developed a large, well-organized army and became the most feared power in the Near East. But the Assyrians had trouble controlling the Babylonian kingdoms, which drove them out of Babylonian territory in 629 B.C.E. Babylonia then turned the tables and attacked Assyria. The Assyrian empire collapsed a short time later, and under King Nebuchadnezzar II Babylonia enjoyed a period of power, wealth, and growth.

THE PERSIAN CONQUEST

Babylonia's newfound glory did not last. It ended when Mesopotamia fell under the control of a powerful eastern neighbor. For centuries the region that is now Iran had been occupied by two warring peoples, the Medes in the north and the Persians in the south. Babylonia had **allied** itself with the Medes in its attack on Assyria. A few years later, however, a Persian king named Cyrus II persuaded Babylonia to join the Persians in a war against the Medes. Cyrus defeated the Medes and claimed their territory—but that was only the start of his plan. He next turned against his Babylonian allies. In 539 B.C.E. Babylonia fell to a Persian army, and soon Cyrus controlled all of Mesopotamia and most of the rest of the Near East. The birthplace of civilization was now a frontier **province** of the sprawling Persian empire.

The Dragon of Marduk decorated a gate in Babylon's city walls. The Neo-Babylonian king Nebuchadnezzar, the conqueror of Jerusalem, built the gate to honor Ishtar, a goddess of love and war. It included many images of this mythical animal, which was sacred to Marduk, the chief god of the city.

CHAPTER TWO

Anatolia:
Cultures of the Crossroads

Anatolia's central plateau is marked by natural outcroppings of rock, which early residents used for building materials. They built some of their stone villages and towns in canyons and on hilltops among the rocks.

WHERE THREE WORLDS MEET

Throughout its long history, Anatolia has been a place where people and cultures have both clashed and blended. Anatolia lies at the meeting place of three worlds: the Near East, the Mediterranean, and central Asia.

Anatolia is the westernmost part of Asia. A high **plateau** ringed with mountains, it juts into the Mediterranean Sea and forms a bridge between Asia and Europe. Only a narrow waterway separates the two continents. West of Anatolia are the Greek islands. Seafarers from ancient Greece could easily reach Anatolia's western coast, where they established colonies. Known to the Greeks as Ionia, the coastal region became part of the Greek world.

On Anatolia's northeastern edge is the Caucasus, the land between the Black and Caspian seas. Migrating tribespeople and armies from central Asia could cross the mountains of the Caucasus to reach Anatolia. To the southeast lie Syria, Mesopotamia, and northern Iran. The ancient civilizations that arose in these

Northwest of Mesopotamia lay Anatolia, another center of ancient Near Eastern civilization. Now the nation of Turkey, Anatolia was home to some of the oldest known human communities. Later, one of the strongest empires of the ancient world would rise there and dominate the Near East for nearly five hundred years.

A merchant holds a scale for weighing goods or payment. Trade was an important part of the Anatolian economy. Four thousand years ago, Anatolian goods—mostly metalwork—were shipped along trade routes to other parts of the Near East.

regions often engaged in trade, alliances, or warfare with the people of Anatolia.

EARLY ANATOLIAN STATES

Some settlements in Anatolia date back to the 8000s B.C.E. Like the Natufians, the people of the earliest settlements gathered their food rather than growing it. By the 6000s B.C.E., however, Anatolians were becoming farmers. Archaeologists have learned much about these early Anatolians by studying the remains of Çatalhöyük, a prehistoric community that existed from about 6300 to 5200 B.C.E.

By 5000 B.C.E. or so, Anatolians lived in a great many small agricultural settlements. Each had a fort or walled castle, often on a hill, to house the local ruler and to shelter people and livestock during raids by rival groups. Beginning around 3000 B.C.E., a few communities grew into larger, more powerful city-states. Some accomplished this by conquering their neighbors, but others grew peacefully, through the migration of people from smaller towns.

TRADE AND WAR

Mesopotamia's wealth lay in its fertile farmlands, while Anatolia's was buried in its rugged mountains rich in copper, silver, iron, gold, and lead. The Anatolians became skilled miners and metalworkers, creating tools, jewelry, armor, and weapons. Merchants from Assyria prized these goods. Before 2000 B.C.E. Assyrian traders developed routes linking Syria and northern Mesopotamia to Anatolia. They also established Assyrian colonies in some of the Anatolian city-states. Goods were not the only things that traveled along the trade routes—languages, customs, and beliefs also entered Anatolia from the south. One especially important influence was the Mesopotamian system of writing, which some Anatolians adopted.

After about 1900 B.C.E., rivalry among the city-states of Anatolia led to centuries of turmoil and war. Each city struggled to gain control of the richest mines and the profitable trade in metals, but their efforts only made commerce dwindle. Conflict closed the trade routes, and foreign merchants stopped coming to Anatolia. Toward the end of this grim period, one group dominated the region and became one of the great powers of the Near East.

THE HITTITE EMPIRE

The Hittites were a people who settled Khatti, in north-central Anatolia. Around

The Many Cities of Troy

The most famous city of ancient Anatolia is Troy. Its fame comes from two Greek epic poems, the *Iliad* and the *Odyssey*, which tell of a war between the Greeks and the Trojans, the people of Troy. Although readers have cherished these poems for several thousand years, most thought that Troy was an imaginary place because the poems are filled with fantastic, unreal locations and creatures. German-born Heinrich Schliemann, however, thought that Troy must have been a real place, and he searched the poems for clues to its location. In 1871 Schliemann began digging into a hill in western Turkey that had long been rumored to be the site of the legendary Troy. He discovered layer upon layer of ruins buried in the hill. When Schliemann unearthed stone pavements, the ruins of a large building, and a wealth of gold jewelry, he believed he had found the legendary city of the *Iliad*.

Today archaeologists still work at the site, which has ten levels of ancient settlements dating from around 3000 B.C.E. to the first two centuries of the Common Era. Scholars cannot say whether or not the Trojan War of the epic poems really happened, but they are

Heinrich Schliemann became famous for discovering the ruins of ancient Troy, a city that many thought was only a legend. Schliemann's methods weren't very scientific, though. Looking for treasure, he cut through the ruins so quickly that one archaeologist grumbled that he was like a dog digging for a bone.

not concerned with proving the truth of old myths. Instead, modern researchers at Troy focus on learning more about the economic and cultural life of the city during its three-thousand-year history.

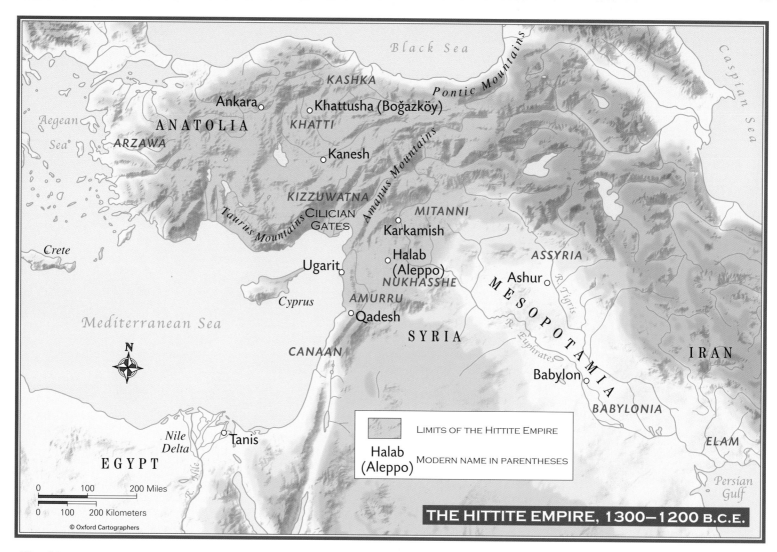

The Hittite empire included most of Anatolia and northern Syria. One of the Hittites' most important conquests was the rich city of Karkamish, on the Euphrates River. Karkamish was a center of the timber trade. Wood passed through it from the Anatolian highlands, shipped on barges down the river to the treeless desert lands of Mesopotamia.

1650 B.C.E. their king established his capital city in a hilltop fortress named Khattusha. He conquered several neighboring states, but it was the next Hittite king, Murshili I, who built an empire by invading and conquering Syria and the faraway city of Babylon.

After Murshili's death, the Hittites lost Babylon and Syria. Other Anatolian states also began attacking the Hittite kingdom. When Shupp-iluliuma I came to the throne in 1380 B.C.E., the Hittites' fortunes improved. They reconquered their restless neighbors, captured the Syrian trade city of Karkamish, and even sent an invading army to Egypt. The Hittite army returned from Egypt victorious, but unfortunately it also brought back a plague that killed the Hittite king.

26

Land of a Thousand Gods

The highlands of Anatolia can be dry and cold at times. Rainfall and the sun's warmth are precious. To the ancient Hittites, the most important deities were the storm god, Teshub, and the sun goddess, Khepat, characters in a myth about a war among the gods. A god named Kumarbi started the war by fighting his own father, the sky god. Afterward Kumarbi fathered Teshub and several other gods, only to be driven away by Teshub. The angry Kumarbi then fathered a monster that threatened to destroy the entire world until Teshub killed both Kumarbi and the monster. The Hittites borrowed the story of Kumarbi and Teshub from the Hurrians, a people who lived in northern Syria and Mesopotamia. Many Hittite gods and myths were borrowed from other cultures—so many that the Hittites claimed to have "a thousand gods." The Hittites also shared the Mesopotamian belief in an underworld where the dead lived in a kingdom ruled by a queen. The Hittites called the underworld the Dark Earth or Gloomy Earth, and they believed that graves, caves, springs, and wells were gateways to this realm. They dug pits to communicate with the gods of the underworld, and they lowered ladders into the pits to help spirits rise to the surface so that they could grant humans favors and join rituals of ancestor worship.

A gold figurine made between 1400 and 1200 B.C.E. represents one of the Hittite gods. Archaeologists know it is a god because of its horned hat. The Mesopotamians pictured their gods wearing headgear with horns. The Hittites borrowed this tradition, just as they borrowed many of their gods from the Mesopotamians and other peoples.

The Hittite empire reached the height of its size and power around 1250 B.C.E., but the end was near. The last Hittite rulers could not fend off attacks from their Anatolian neighbors, invasions by bands from eastern Europe, and revolts within the empire. In about 1190, an invading army entered Khatti. It burned Khattusha, and the Hittite empire went up in smoke.

PHRYGIA AND LYDIA

After the fall of the Hittites, Anatolia became once again a region of many small warring states. Around 1000 B.C.E., one of those states, Phrygia, gained control of west-central Anatolia. Much of what we know about Phrygia comes from the Greeks, who began founding their colonies in Ionia at this time. The most famous ruler of Phrygia was Midas, who married a Greek woman. Midas sought help from the Assyrians in fighting off the Cimmerians, mounted warriors from southern Russia who had surged across the Caucasus. The Assyrians didn't help, and around 700 B.C.E. the Cimmerians burned Midas's capital, Gordium. Legend says the king killed himself rather than face defeat.

The Cimmerians were nomads who did not linger in the cities they conquered and

A Lydian coin from the 600s B.C.E. Coins of this period were made of electrum, a blend of gold and silver. Workers who minted the money used a stamp to press the same design into each coin.

looted. They left western Anatolia, making way for a new power to rise. That power was the kingdom of Lydia, famous throughout the ancient world for its wealth (and known to modern archaeologists as the first society to create and use coins). Eastern Anatolia, meanwhile, was dominated by a kingdom called Urartu, which fought a long series of wars with Assyria. But like Mesopotamia, Anatolia was soon swallowed up by the Persian empire. Persia seized Anatolia around 547 B.C.E., and although the Persians let some local kings remain on their thrones, these puppet rulers had no real power.

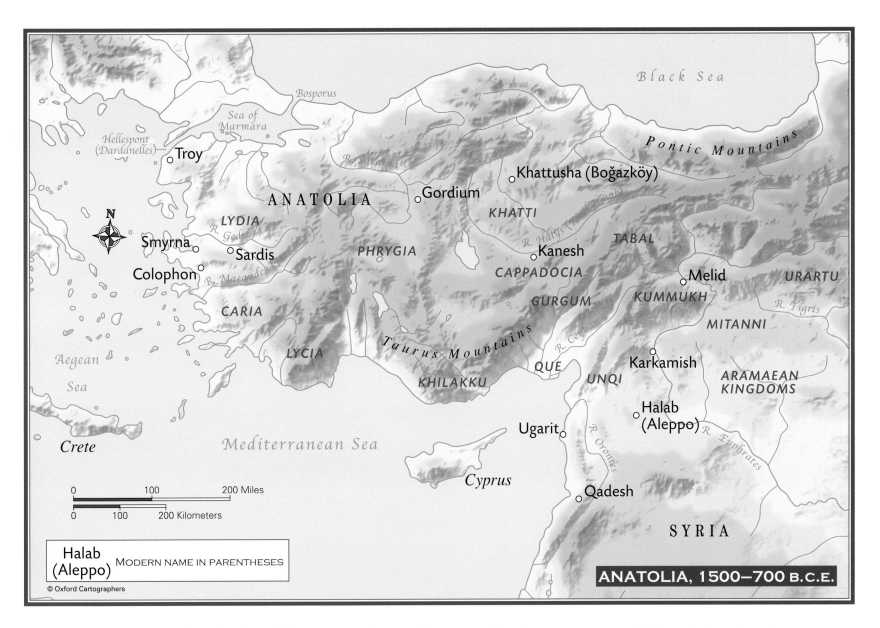

ANATOLIA, 1500–700 B.C.E.

Black Sea

Bosporus

Sea of Marmara

Hellespont (Dardanelles)

Troy

ANATOLIA

Pontic Mountains

Khattusha (Boğazköy)

Gordium

KHATTI

LYDIA

Smyrna

Sardis

Colophon

R. Gedi

R. Maeander

PHRYGIA

R. Halys

Kanesh

TABAL

CAPPADOCIA

GURGUM

KUMMUKH

Melid

URARTU

R. Tigris

MITANNI

CARIA

LYCIA

Taurus Mountains

R. Ceyhan

QUE

Karkamish

ARAMAEAN KINGDOMS

KHILAKKU

UNQI

Aegean Sea

Halab (Aleppo)

R. Euphrates

Ugarit

R. Orontes

Crete

Mediterranean Sea

Cyprus

Qadesh

SYRIA

0   100   200 Miles

0   100   200 Kilometers

Halab (Aleppo)   MODERN NAME IN PARENTHESES

© Oxford Cartographers

The Hittites, whose homeland was Khatti, were only one of many peoples who came to power in Anatolia in ancient times. After the Hittite empire collapsed, the Phrygians dominated central Anatolia, and the Urartians took control of the mountainous region to the east. In 715 B.C.E. the Assyrian king Sargon II defeated King Rusa I of Urartu in battle. The Assyrians looted the Urartian kingdom but could not control its fiercely independent people, who soon drove them out. Both Phrygia and Urartu finally fell into the hands of the Cimmerians, horsemen who swept across the Caucasus Mountains from Russia.

Egypt:
Land of the River

In some ways, Egypt today is much like the ancient kingdom of the pharaohs: a ribbon of green farmland through which its lifeline, the Nile River, flows.

BEFORE THE PHARAOHS

Egypt is a long narrow ribbon of fertile land along the Nile River, with desert on both sides. Its first inhabitants were nomads who not only hunted and gathered wild foods but also fished the river. Later, when they began practicing agriculture, the river remained vital to their lives. It supplied their fields with water and brought rich new soil during its yearly floods. The river defined Egypt's three main inhabited areas. The delta, the marshy region where the Nile breaks into several smaller channels as it empties into the Mediterranean, is Lower Egypt. The river south of the delta is Upper Egypt. The third region, the Faiyûm Depression, is a low-lying area southwest of the delta watered by a branch of the Nile.

After about 5000 B.C.E. the Egyptians lived in many small communities, some of which eventually became local kingdoms. During the 3000s the Egyptians began receiving trade goods from southern

The civilization that developed in ancient Egypt is famous for its massive stone monuments and for the splendidly decorated tombs of its pharaohs, or kings. But perhaps the most impressive thing about ancient Egypt is that its civilization endured for nearly three thousand years with few of the dramatic political changes that affected Mesopotamia and Anatolia.

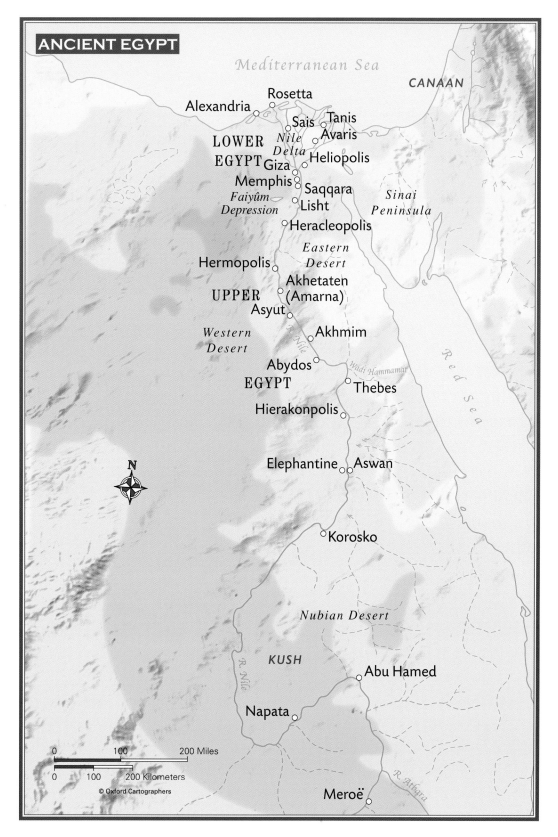

ANCIENT EGYPT

Mediterranean Sea

CANAAN

Rosetta
Alexandria
Sais   Tanis
Avaris
LOWER   *Nile*
EGYPT   *Delta*   Heliopolis
Giza
Memphis   Saqqara
Faiyûm   Lisht
Depression
Heracleopolis

Eastern
Desert
Hermopolis
Akhetaten
UPPER   (Amarna)
Asyut
Western   Akhmim
Desert
Abydos
EGYPT   Thebes
Hierakonpolis

Sinai
Peninsula

Wadi Hammamat

Red Sea

N

Elephantine Aswan

Korosko

Nubian Desert

KUSH   Abu Hamed
R. Nile
Napata

R. Atbara

Meroë

0   100   200 Miles
0   100   200 Kilometers
© Oxford Cartographers

People and goods could easily move through Lower and Upper Egypt by boat along the Nile. But south of Elephantine a series of rapids made water travel much more difficult. Still, the Egyptians sent traders and armies into the lands south of their borders. Pharaohs of the Old Kingdom conquered Nubia, the region around the city of Meroë. Nubia later regained its independence and survived as a kingdom until 350 C.E.

The first pyramid, sometimes called the step pyramid, was built to house the tomb of King Djoser, who ruled Egypt from 2630 to 2611 B.C.E.

Mesopotamia. They also developed their own style of writing, perhaps inspired by the written language of the Sumerians.

One of the most important events in Egypt's history took place around 3000 B.C.E., when Menes, ruler of a kingdom in Upper Egypt, managed to conquer the rest of the country. For the first time, Egypt was united under a single ruler. Menes founded Egypt's First **Dynasty** and set up his capital at Memphis, at the boundary between Lower and Upper Egypt, so that he could oversee the entire country.

THE OLD KINGDOM

When Egypt's Third Dynasty came to power in 2675 B.C.E., Egypt entered what historians call the Old Kingdom period.

It lasted about five hundred years and was a time of wealth, strict government control of the population, and ambitious building programs. The grandest of these projects involved tombs. For centuries Egyptians had been burying their dead in mastabas—low mounds of stone or sun-dried clay bricks. The mastabas were meant to preserve the bodies of the dead because Egyptians believed that their spirits could not survive in the afterlife unless their bodies remained whole.

Over time, the tombs of kings and other high officials became larger and more elaborate, with inner rooms filled with the treasures and everyday possessions of the dead. Early in the Old Kingdom, an architect named Imhotep enlarged the mastaba that was being built

The Great Stone Face

At Giza, near Cairo, Egypt, great pyramids of stone rise majestically from the desert, their steep, sloping sides outlined sharply against the sky. Among them crouches another shape, a stone lion 240 feet (73 m) long. Its head, 65 feet (20 m) high, is that of a man. Archaeologists think that this Great Sphinx dates from the reign of Khufu, an Old Kingdom pharaoh who ruled from 2585 to 2560 B.C.E. The Egyptians made other sphinxes, usually with lions' bodies and men's heads, but sometimes with rams' heads or crocodiles' tails. Sphinxes were symbols of divine power, representing both the god Amon and the ruling pharaoh.

Some descriptions of ancient Egypt do not mention the Great Sphinx. This is because it was often covered by the shifting sands of the desert. Today the massive sculpture is still the source of myths and legends. One modern legend says that the sphinx's missing nose was shot off by a cannon of French general Napoléon Bonaparte, who invaded Egypt in 1798 (not true—the nose was missing long before the French arrived). Other modern myths, equally imaginary, try to link the sphinx with alien visitors, mystical secret powers of the ancients (such as the ability to move rocks with mind control), and other odd and unproven notions.

A photograph of the Great Sphinx from the late 1800s. For centuries, travelers to Egypt have been fascinated by the broken but still noble features of this stone being, who wears a royal headdress. Many historians think that the features are those of the pharaoh Khufu or his son Chephren.

for King Djoser. He added layers like steps, each smaller than the one below it, to a height of 200 feet (61 m). The result was the first pyramid. Later rulers made larger pyramids, most of which had straight sides instead of steps. The largest was the Great Pyramid at Giza, not far from Memphis. It reached a height of 480 feet (146 m) and was built for King Khufu, who died in 2560 B.C.E. Khufu's son and grandson built their own pyramids at Giza—today the three structures are recognized all over the world as symbols of Egypt.

After about 2200 B.C.E., the Old Kingdom declined. Local leaders grew impatient with the central government and began setting up their own kingdoms. At the same time, **droughts** caused **famines** that plunged Egypt into disorder. The once-powerful central government collapsed, leaving rival kingdoms and dynasties to wage civil war.

THE MIDDLE KINGDOM

The unrest caused by the collapse of the Old Kingdom ended in 2040 B.C.E., when the king of Thebes, in Upper Egypt, managed to conquer Lower Egypt.

The 350 years that followed are known as the Middle Kingdom. Once again the land was united under a single ruler, but this time its capital was at Thebes. With the seat of power located far to the south in Upper Egypt, the pharaohs turned their attention in that direction and conquered Nubia, on Egypt's southern border (in present-day Sudan). By 1990 B.C.E., however, the first pharaoh of the Twelfth Dynasty had moved the capital to a site near Memphis.

The Middle Kingdom carried on a lively trade with the city-states of the Levant, and many people from western Asia settled in Egypt. The Middle Kingdom was also a time of great literary activity. Egypt's written language consisted of marks called hieroglyphs made on papyrus, a paperlike substance made from reeds. Writings from the Old Kingdom deal mainly with accounting, the storage of goods, and other records, but during the Middle Kingdom scribes began recording Egypt's myths, stories, history, and poetry.

During the 1700s B.C.E., central rule once again collapsed. Egypt was governed by two rival dynasties, one from Memphis and the other from the eastern part of the

The pyramids at Giza are much larger than the step pyramid, and they contain complex networks of tunnels and chambers. The ancient Greek historian Herodotus wrote that it took 100,000 men as long as 20 years to build each of the three largest pyramids. Some modern experts claim that Herodotus was mistaken—or perhaps exaggerating on purpose. They think that 20,000 workers could have built the largest pyramid in about 6 years.

delta. This division of power weakened Egypt's defenses, and an outside enemy overwhelmed both ruling houses. The Hyksos, a people from Syria or the southern Levant, captured Memphis and gained control of Egypt around 1630 B.C.E.

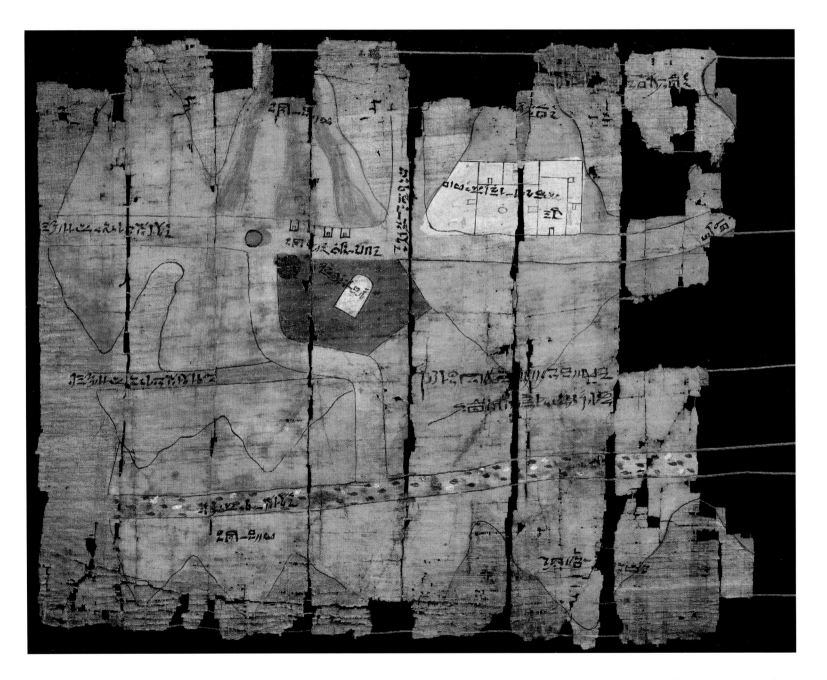

A fragment of papyrus from around 1100 B.C.E. shows that the ancient Egyptians were mapmakers. This map records the location of some of the mines that yielded gold for many of the magnificant objects found in the tombs of the pharaohs.

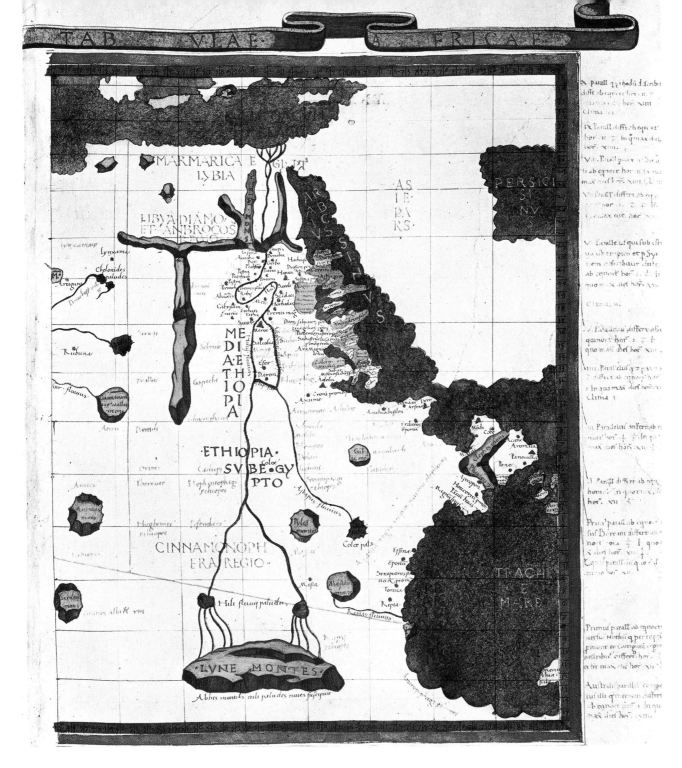

This map of Egypt made around 1470 C.E. is based on the geography of Ptolemy, an ancient Greek scholar from Alexandria, at the mouth of the Nile River. The map also shows Ethiopia, including the ancient land of Nubia. Ptolemy claimed that the mighty Nile flowed out of two lakes fed by streams from a range he called the Mountains of the Moon. His notions of geography endured for centuries. In the 1800s, explorers from many European nations probed central Africa in a quest to find the lakes, the mountains, and the source of the Nile.

During his reign, Akhenaten did much to change the art and religion of Egypt. He encouraged the worship of a new form of sun god in reviving a little-known deity named Aton. His broad, sweeping changes also inspired new styles of art, no longer depicting scenes of the afterlife but day-to-day portrayals of the king eating or sharing a tender moment with his wife, Nefertiti.

THE NEW KINGDOM

Ahmose I, founder of the Eighteenth Dynasty, overthrew the Hyksos and drove them out of Egypt around 1530 B.C.E. His reign marked the beginning of the New Kingdom, Egypt's third period of central rule. Many New Kingdom pharaohs left their mark on history. Thutmose III conquered terri-

tory in western Asia as far north as Syria. Akhenaten led a religious movement that called for the worship of a single sun god instead of Egypt's many traditional deities. The new religion did not last long, however, because the powerful priests of Egypt's temples resented it and forbade its practice after Akhenaten's death. The pharaoh Tutankhamen is best remembered today because his tomb, discovered in 1922 C.E., is the most magnificent ever found. The last powerful pharaoh of the New Kingdom was Ramses II, who ruled for nearly seventy years and filled Egypt with monuments, including many enormous statues of himself. During the century after Ramses's death, the New Kingdom began to crumble. By 1075 B.C.E., it fell apart, once more leaving Egypt divided among numerous local rulers.

FOREIGN RULERS

The end of the New Kingdom left Egypt weak and open to invasion. For a time it was ruled by foreign dynasties: first Libyans from the desert on Egypt's western border and then Nubians from the south. The Nubian dynasty ended around 656

Simple affection in a splendid setting. An image of the pharaoh Tutankhamen and his wife, found in his tomb many centuries after his death, is a window into the lives of the royal couple.

Hatshepsut, a Female Pharaoh

Only four women ever ruled ancient Egypt. The most powerful and best known was Hatshepsut, a queen who named herself king. Hatshepsut was the daughter of Thutmose I, a pharaoh of the New Kingdom. Following the custom of Egyptian royal families, she married her half brother, who in time became the pharaoh Thutmose II. They had a daughter but no son. Around 1479 B.C.E. Thutmose II died. His son by another woman was supposed to become the next pharaoh, but he was too young to take the throne, so his stepmother, Hatshepsut, served as regent (someone who rules temporarily on behalf of someone else). She used her position as regent to win friends among the officials of the court and the temples. Then, in 1472, Hatshepsut arranged for the priests of the god Amon to declare that the deity wanted Hatshepsut to be the true ruler of Egypt. She stopped calling herself queen and took the title pharaoh. Artwork of the time shows her wearing the robes, crown, and traditional false beard of a pharaoh. Hatshepsut ruled Egypt as pharaoh until her death in 1458 B.C.E., although she allowed Thutmose III, her stepson, to be called pharaoh at the same time.

Many images of Hatshepsut show her wearing a man's beard, a symbol of the ruler's power. But this granite statue clearly shows her as a woman, one of only four to rule ancient Egypt.

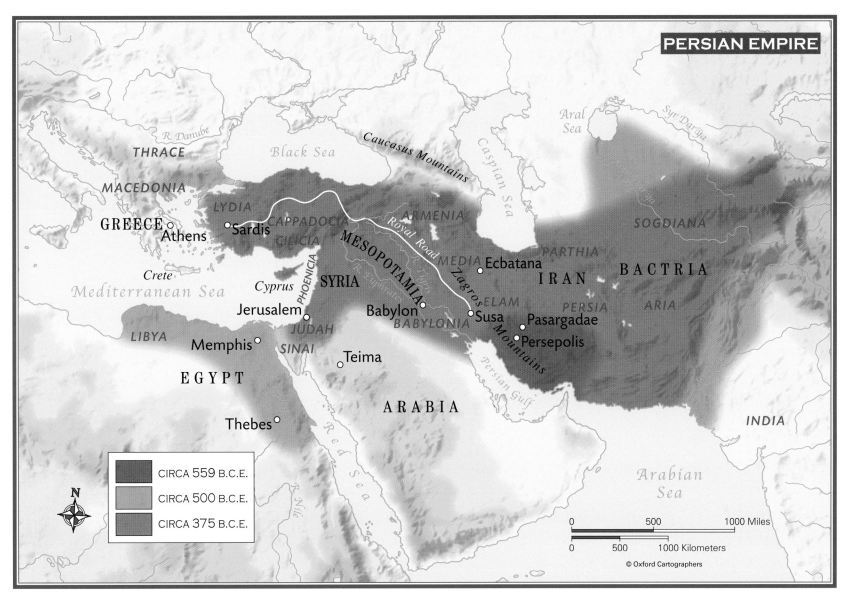

The Persian empire, based in what is now Iran, spread out from its capital city of Persepolis. At its height, around 500 B.C.E., the empire ruled the entire Near East, including the ancient lands of Mesopotamia, Anatolia, and Egypt. But just as these lands had fallen to the Persians, the Persian empire would one day fall to an invader from across the sea—Alexander the Great, king of Macedon and Greece.

B.C.E. when Assyria invaded and conquered Egypt. The conquerers allowed native Egyptian rulers to govern the land—under Assyrian control, of course. One of these local kings soon threw off Assyrian rule and managed to unite Egypt under a single pharaoh for the last time. His dynasty, the twenty-sixth, survived for a century. In 525, the Egyptian empire came to an end, facing the same fate as the civilizations of ancient Mesopotamia and Anatolia: it was conquered by the Persians.

Glossary

allied—Formed an alliance, or agreement, to help one another or to work together for a common goal.

archaeologist—One who studies ancient civilizations and cultures, usually by digging up ruins.

deity—A god or goddess.

drought—A period of unusually low rainfall or water level.

dynasty—A series of rulers from the same family or group.

empire—A large political organization that contains more than one cultural group or language; usually created by force.

famine—A severe food shortage.

nomads—People who move from place to place instead of living in permanent settlements.

plateau—A fairly flat landscape above sea level.

province—A part of a nation or empire; a region that does not govern itself but is subject to outside rule.

scribe—One whose job is to read, write, and keep records.

urban—Having to do with cities or city life.

10,000 Natufian culture appears in the Levant.

9000 People in the Levant begin farming.

8000s Permanent settlements appear in Anatolia and at the site of what may be the world's oldest town—Jericho in present-day Jordan.

7000 Permanent settlements appear in northern Mesopotamia and Persia (present-day Iran).

5200 Permanent settlements appear in northern Egypt.

4000–3000 Mesopotamian peoples form city-states and develop writing. Egyptians also develop writing.

3000 Egypt is unified into a single kingdom under a ruler named Menes.

3000–2200 City-states appear in Anatolia. The Sumerian state and the Akkadian empire emerge in Mesopotamia.

2675–2130 Egypt is ruled by pharaohs of the Old Kingdom.

2200–1600 The Hittites rise to power in Anatolia. In Mesopotamia the Assyrian and Babylonian empires also become powerful.

2040–1630 Pharaohs of the Middle Kingdom rule Egypt, which is invaded by the Hyksos around 1630.

1600–1200 After reaching its peak in Anatolia, the Hittite empire wages war on Egypt and Mesopotamia and then collapses. The Babylonian and Assyrian states survive.

1530–1075 Egypt is ruled by pharaohs of the New Kingdom.

1200–500 The Babylonian and Assyrian states enter their late periods. Small kingdoms emerge in Anatolia.

1075–332 Various Egyptian dynasties and foreign powers struggle for control of Egypt.

500s–331 The Persians conquer Babylonia, Egypt, and part of Anatolia, which are added to the Persian empire.

Chronology

(all dates are B.C.E.)

Further Reading

BOOKS

Anatolia: Cauldron of Cultures. Alexandria, VA: Time-Life Books, 1995.

Bauman, Hans. *In the Land of Ur: The Discovery of Ancient Mesopotamia.* Stella Humphries, translator. New York: Pantheon Books, 1969.

Corbishley, M. J. *The Near East.* Hemel Hempstead, England: Macdonald Young Books, 1995.

Egypt: Land of the Pharaohs. Alexandria, VA: Time-Life Books, 1992.

Epics of Early Civilization: Middle Eastern Myth. Alexandria, VA: Time-Life Books, 2000.

Haynes, Joyce L. *Egyptian Dynasties.* New York: Franklin Watts, 1998.

Haywood, John. *The Encyclopedia of Ancient Civilizations of the Near East and Mediterranean.* Armonk, NY: Sharpe Reference, 1997.

The Holy Land. Alexandria, VA: Time-Life Books, 1992.

Hunter, Erica. *First Civilizations.* New York: Facts On File, 2003, revised edition.

Mesopotamia: The Mighty Kings. Alexandria, VA: Time-Life Books, 1995.

Nardo, Don. *Ancient Egypt.* San Diego: Kidhaven Press, 2002.

Odijk, Pamela. *The Sumerians.* Englewood Cliffs, NJ: Silver Burdett Press, 1990.

Perl, Lila. *Mummies, Tombs, and Treasure: Secrets of Ancient Egypt.* New York: Clarion Books, 1987.

Sumer: Cities of Eden. Alexandria, VA: Time-Life Books, 1994.

Wallenfels, Ronald, ed. *The Ancient Near East: An Encyclopedia for Students.* 4 vols. New York: Scribner, 2000.

What Life Was Like on the Banks of the Nile: Egypt, 3050–30 B.C. Alexandria, VA: Time-Life Books, 1997.

WEB SITES

www.carlos.emory.edu/ODYSSEY/NEAREAST/ homepg.html
The Near East-Cradle of Civilization, maintained by Emory University's Michael C. Carlos Museum, has sections on Egypt and the Near East that explore archaeology, people, mythology, daily life, death and burial, and other topics.

www.ce.eng.usf.edu/pharos/wonders/
This site is devoted to the Seven Wonders of the Ancient World, some of which were located in the Near East.

www.asor.org/HITTITE/HittiteHP.html
The Hittite home page offers a wide range of information about the Hittites and other peoples of the ancient Near East.

www.smm.org/catal/toc/htm
Designed for students and young people, the Mysteries of Çatalhöyük page is an interactive introduction to discoveries made at an archaeological site in Anatolia (modern Turkey).

www.dia.org/collections/ancient/mesopotamia/ mesopotamia.html
The Detroit Institute of Arts offers examples of artwork from ancient Mesopotamia.

www.carnegiemuseums.org/cmnh/exhibits/ egypt/
This Carnegie Museum of Natural History site contains sections on the history, daily life, and gods and religion of ancient Egypt, as well as other topics.

ABOUT THE AUTHOR

Rebecca Stefoff is the author of Marshall Cavendish's North American Historical Atlases series, the *Young Oxford Companion to Maps and Mapmaking,* and many other nonfiction books for children and young adults. History, geography, and maps are among her special interests. She makes her home in Portland, Oregon. Find out more about her books at www.rebeccastefoff.com.

Index